Your Blood

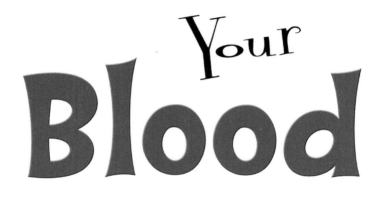

How Your BODY Works

Your Blood

Anita Ganeri

Gareth Stevens Publishing
A WORLD ALMANAC EDUCATION GROUP COMPANY

ACKNOWLEDGMENTS

With thanks to: Sara Velmi, Max Wybourn, Jake Clark, Mia Powell, Lauren Chapple, Courtney Thomas, Bethan Matthews, Skye Johnson, and Ellen and Jack Millard. Models from The Norrie Carr Agency and Truly Scrumptious Ltd.

Please visit our web site at: www.garethstevens.com
For a free color catalog describing Gareth Stevens Publishing's
list of high-quality books and multimedia programs, call
1-800-542-2595 (USA) or 1-800-387-3178 (Canada).
Gareth Stevens Publishing's fax: (414) 332-3567.

Library of Congress Cataloging-in-Publication Data

Ganeri, Anita, 1961-
  Your blood / by Anita Ganeri.
    p. cm. — (How your body works)
  Summary: An introduction to the human heart, blood, blood vessels, and various types of blood cells.
  Includes bibliographical references and index.
  ISBN 0-8368-3631-6 (lib. bdg.)
  1. Blood—Juvenile literature. [1. Blood.] I. Title. II. Series.
  QP91.G166   2003
  612.1'1—dc21   2002036527

This North American edition first published in 2003 by
Gareth Stevens Publishing
A World Almanac Education Group Company
330 West Olive Street, Suite 100
Milwaukee, WI 53212 USA

Original edition © 2003 by Evans Brothers Limited. First published in 2003 by Evans Brothers Limited, 2A Portman Mansions, Chiltern Street, London W1U 6NR, United Kingdom. This U.S. edition published under license from Evans Brothers Limited. This U.S. edition © 2003 by Gareth Stevens, Inc. Additional end matter © 2003 by Gareth Stevens, Inc.

Designer: Mark Holt
Artwork: Julian Baker
Photography: Steve Shott
Consultant: Dr. M. Turner

Gareth Stevens Editor: Carol Ryback
Gareth Stevens Designer: Katherine A. Goedheer

Photo credits:
Science Photo Library: National Cancer Institute, page 9; Professors P. M. Motta and S. Correr, page 10; Alfred Pasieka, page 13; Damien Lovegrove, page 15. Bruce Coleman Collection, page 21.

Printed in the United States of America

1 2 3 4 5 6 7 8 9 07 06 05 04 03

Contents

Blood-Red Blood

A very special liquid is always moving through your body. What is it? Blood! Blood is the red, sticky liquid that comes out of you when you cut yourself. Your blood carries useful things to every part of your body. It carries oxygen from the air you breathe and **nutrients** from the food you eat. It also collects waste, such as carbon dioxide gas, and helps your body fight **germs**.

When you were born, you had about two mugfuls of blood in your body. An adult has about ten mugfuls of blood.

Your blood cannot move through your body without help. It is pushed around your body by a very strong muscle in your chest. This muscle is called your heart. Each time your amazing heart beats, it moves blood around your body through lots of soft tubes called **blood vessels**. Your heart beats day and night to keep blood moving through your body.

Amazing!

Your blood, heart, and blood vessels are called your **circulatory system**. "Circulatory" means traveling in a circle, around and around without a beginning or an end.

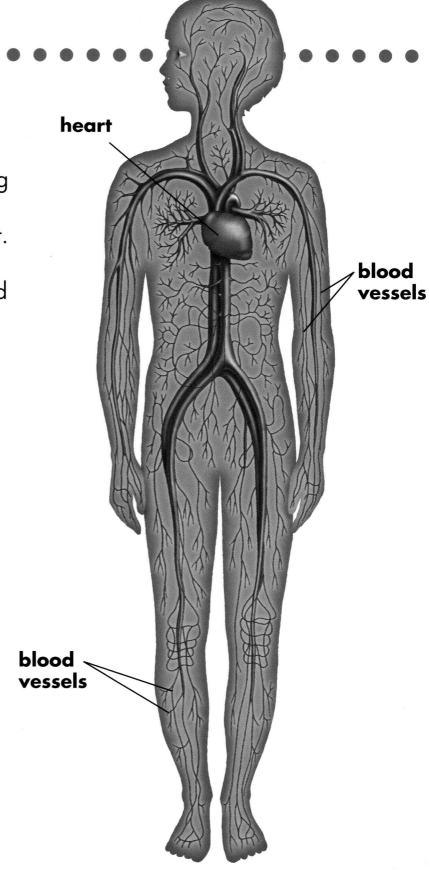

heart

blood vessels

blood vessels

What Is Blood?

More than half of your blood is a watery fluid called **plasma**. The rest of your blood is made of tiny pieces of solid material called blood cells. Blood cells carry oxygen and nutrients through your body. If you looked at a drop of blood under a **microscope**, you would see different kinds of blood cells.

To see what blood cells floating in plasma look like, put crushed tea leaves into sugar water and shake them up.

Your blood has **red blood cells** and **white blood cells**. Red blood cells carry oxygen and other gases around your body. White blood cells help fight any germs in your blood. **Platelets** are tiny pieces of cells floating in the plasma. Platelets help stop the bleeding when you cut yourself.

Amazing!

You have about 2,000,000 red blood cells, 5,000 white blood cells, and 250,000 platelets in each drop of your blood.

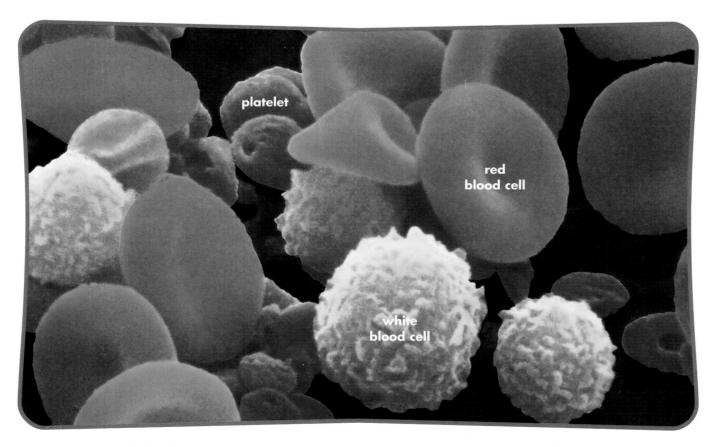

Your blood's watery plasma carries red blood cells, white blood cells, and platelets throughout your body.

Red Blood Cells

Red blood cells look like tiny doughnuts without holes. Your blood has billions and billions of them, more than any other type of body cell. Red blood cells give your blood its red color.

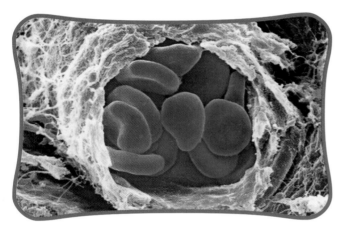

Red blood cells are so tiny that many can fit inside a blood vessel at once.

Amazing!

Your body is always making new red blood cells. Each red blood cell lives about four months and travels around your body over 150,000 times.

Red blood cells get their red color from the **hemoglobin** (HEEM–oh–gloh–bin) they carry. Hemoglobin is a chemical that turns bright red when it picks up oxygen. As your blood travels through your lungs, oxygen from the air you breathe sticks to the hemoglobin in your red blood cells. Now your bright red blood can carry the oxygen around your body. As your body uses the oxygen, your blood changes color and becomes a very dark red.

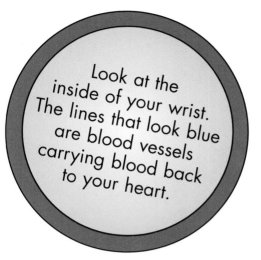

Look at the inside of your wrist. The lines that look blue are blood vessels carrying blood back to your heart.

White Blood Cells

White blood cells look white because they do not carry hemoglobin. Your white blood cells are a little larger than your red blood cells. Your blood has fewer white blood cells than red blood cells. White blood cells also have a different job than red blood cells. Your white blood cells help your body fight germs that cause illnesses.

When your body temperature is too high, you have a fever. A fever means that your white blood cells are fighting germs in your body.

Germs get into your body through your nose and mouth or through cuts on your skin. Inside your body, the germs grow and attack your cells. As your body starts to fight the germs, you may have **symptoms**, such as fever, aches and pains, or just feeling sick.

Some white blood cells surround germs and gobble them up whole. Other white blood cells make chemicals that stick to germs and kill them. White blood cells make thousands of different kinds of chemicals to protect your body against different kinds of germs.

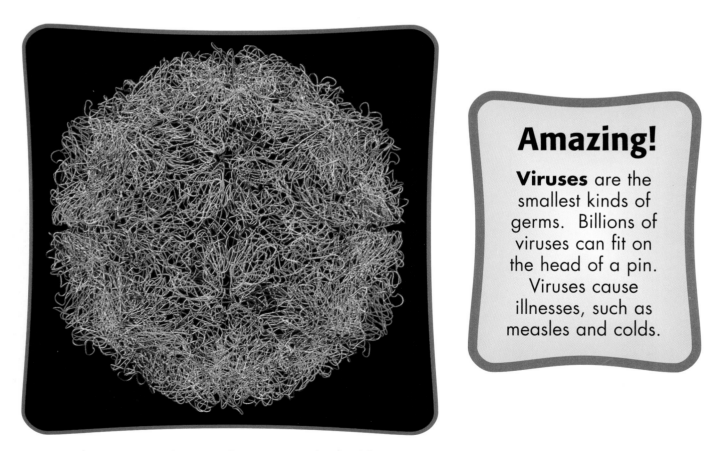

This picture shows what a virus looks like through a microscope. This virus might cause you to catch a cold.

Amazing!

Viruses are the smallest kinds of germs. Billions of viruses can fit on the head of a pin. Viruses cause illnesses, such as measles and colds.

Plasma and Platelets

About half of your blood is a pale, yellowish liquid called plasma. Your blood cells float in it. Plasma is mostly water, but it also carries nutrients and waste from the food you eat. Your body uses nutrients to grow and repair itself. Nutrients also give you energy.

You can use a bandage as extra protection to keep a cut clean.

Platelets are tiny pieces of cells that are even smaller than red blood cells. They help form blood **clots**, which stop the bleeding when you cut yourself. Dried blood and platelets form a tough scab to protect the cut and help it heal.

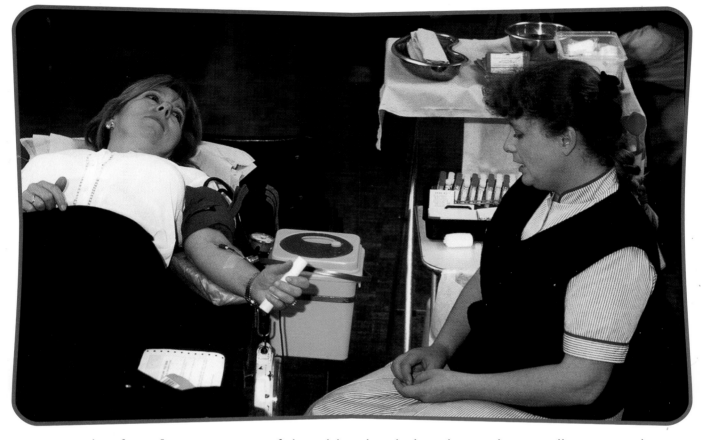

People often **donate** some of their blood to help others who are ill or injured.

Your blood belongs to one of four blood groups. The groups are called type O, type A, type B, and type AB. Your **blood type** depends on special chemicals in your blood cells and plasma. Doctors can test your blood to find out which blood type you have in your body.

Amazing!

Some sick or injured people may need a **blood transfusion** to get better. The blood they receive must match their own blood type.

Blood Vessels

Your blood travels around your body in thin tubes called blood vessels. **Arteries** are blood vessels that carry blood from your heart to the rest of your body. Arteries have thick, stretchy walls. The walls stretch so the force of blood flowing through your arteries will not break them.

If you look in a mirror and gently pull down your lower eyelid, you will see some of the tiniest blood vessels in your body.

Blood vessels become smaller and smaller until they are too tiny to see. The tiniest blood vessels are called **capillaries**. Capillaries have very thin walls so that oxygen and nutrients can move out of your blood and into your body **tissues**. Every tissue in your body has capillaries.

Capillaries can be arteries or **veins**. Veins are blood vessels that carry blood back to your heart. They have tiny flaps, called **valves**, that stop your blood from flowing backward.

Amazing!

If you could stretch out all your blood vessels, they would reach around Earth twice.

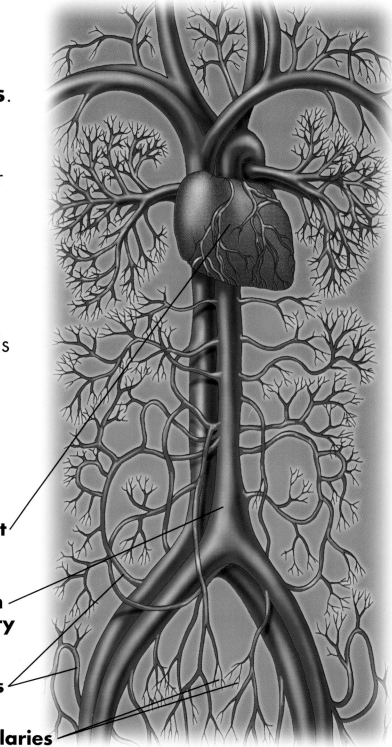

heart

main artery

veins

capillaries

Have a Heart

• •

Your heart sits in the middle of your chest, slightly to the left, between your two lungs. Day and night, your heart pumps blood around your body. Your amazing heart will pump blood all your life.

Your heart was about the size of a walnut when you were born. Now your heart is about the size of your fist.

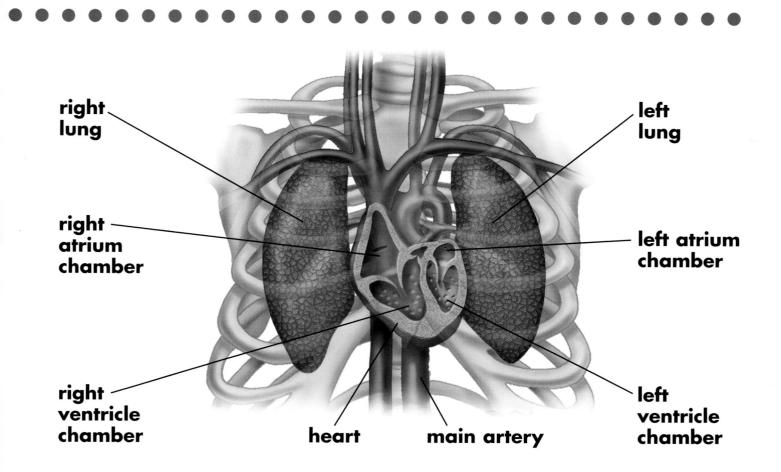

right lung

right atrium chamber

right ventricle chamber

left lung

left atrium chamber

left ventricle chamber

heart   main artery

Your heart is a special muscle that never gets tired. It has four parts, or chambers. The top chambers are called the right **atrium** and the left atrium. The bottom chambers are called the right **ventricle** and the left ventricle. Thick flaps called valves connect the top chambers with the bottom chambers. Your heart squeezes the chambers in a certain order to pump blood to every part of your body.

Amazing!

Your heart grows in size until you become an adult. A healthy heart will always be about the same size as your fist.

Heartbeat

Each pump of your heart is called a **heartbeat**. Every heartbeat moves blood from your body into the right side of your heart. The right side of your heart pumps the blood to your lungs for a fresh supply of oxygen. The blood from your lungs flows to the left side of your heart. The left side of your heart pumps your blood through your many blood vessels to all parts of your body.

Amazing!

Your blood always travels around your body in the same direction. It takes about forty-five seconds for one trip.

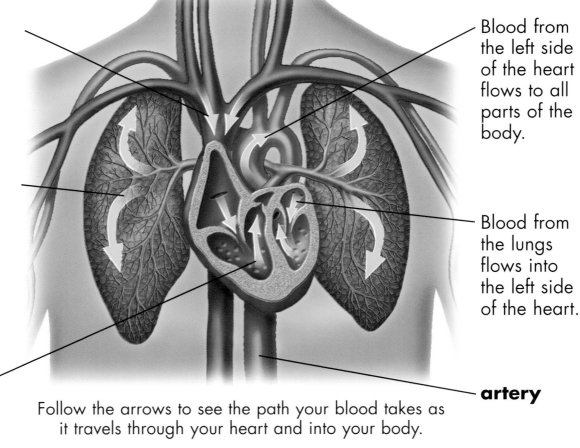

Blood from the body flows into the right side of the heart.

Blood from the right side of the heart flows into the lungs.

Blood from the left side of the heart flows to all parts of the body.

Blood from the lungs flows into the left side of the heart.

heart

artery

Follow the arrows to see the path your blood takes as it travels through your heart and into your body.

An elephant's heart beats very slowly.

The valves between your heart chambers must open to let blood flow through. Then they quickly snap shut to keep your blood from flowing backward. The snapping valves make the sound you hear as a heartbeat. A doctor or nurse listens to your heartbeat using an instrument called a **stethoscope**.

Amazing!

A huge elephant's heart beats about twenty-five times a minute. A tiny shrew's heart beats an amazing six hundred times a minute.

Fast and Slow

Your heart must beat all the time, or your body would die. But you do not think about your heart beating. Your amazing heart beats automatically — about eighty times a minute, which is more than 100,000 times a day. Each beat pumps blood out of your heart and around your body. You can feel this blood movement as a throbbing, or **pulse**, in your wrist.

Press your fingers on your wrist, just below your thumb. Can you feel your wrist throbbing? This throbbing is your pulse.

The number of times your heart beats in one minute depends on what you are doing. Exercise makes your heart beat faster, because your muscles are working hard and need lots of food and oxygen to keep moving. Sleeping makes your heart beat slower, because your muscles are resting and need less food and oxygen to lie quietly.

If you put your hand on your chest after you stop running, you will feel your heart beating very fast.

Healthy Heart

Some people's hearts do not work properly. Sometimes, the blood vessels in a person's heart become blocked up, and blood cannot get through to the heart muscles. When blood cannot get through, the heart stops beating, which causes a **heart attack**. If your heart stops beating, you can die in about four minutes. Ambulances and hospitals have special machines that can make a heart start beating again.

Jumping rope is an exercise that makes your muscles work hard and your heart beat fast. Exercise is good for your heart.

Some people are born with weak hearts, or their heart becomes sick. Smoking, eating too much, and not exercising can also make a heart become weak or sick. The best way to keep your heart healthy is to eat nutritious food and exercise regularly. Eating right and exercising help keep your amazing heart fit and strong throughout your life.

Amazing!

An operation called a **heart transplant** replaces a sick heart with a healthy heart.

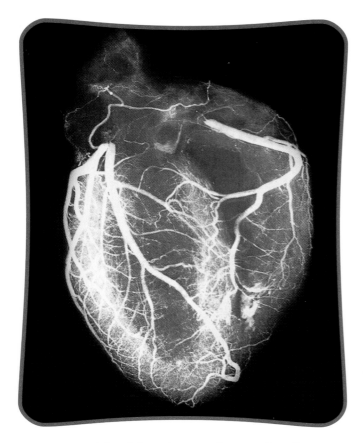

Healthy blood vessels reach all areas of the heart muscle.

A blocked blood vessel can cause a heart attack.

Activity

● ●

Your circulatory system has different parts. How many parts can you name? Photocopy page 27 and match the numbers below to the body parts listed on page 27.

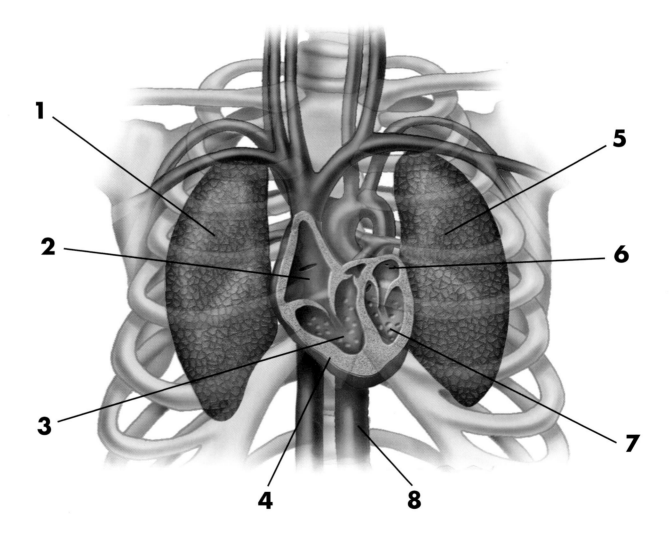

Do not write on this page! Ask an adult to help you photocopy this page, then write your answers on the photocopy. (See page 19 to check your answers.)

____ **main artery**

____ **left atrium chamber**

____ **left lung**

____ **right ventricle chamber**

____ **right atrium chamber**

____ **heart**

____ **right lung**

____ **left ventricle chamber**

Glossary

arteries: blood vessels that carry blood from the heart to the rest of your body.

atrium: one of the two upper chambers of your heart.

blood transfusion: adding new, healthy blood to a sick or injured person's body through a blood vessel in his or her arm.

blood type: one of the four different blood groups.

blood vessels: tiny tubes that carry blood to all parts of your body.

capillaries: the tiniest blood vessels in your body.

circulatory system: the network formed by your heart and your blood vessels that keeps blood traveling around and around your body.

clots: clumps of platelets and other blood cells inside a blood vessel that stops blood from flowing.

donate: to give away blood or other objects for free.

germs: tiny living things that cause some illnesses.

heart attack: a stopped heartbeat caused by a blocked blood vessel in your heart.

heart transplant: an operation that replaces a sick heart with a healthy heart.

heartbeat: the "thub-dub" you hear when your heart valves snap closed.

hemoglobin: a chemical in red blood cells that carries oxygen, which gives blood its bright red color.

microscope: an instrument used to look at objects that are too tiny to see with just your eyes.

nutrients: the healthy parts of food your blood carries around your body.

plasma: the clear, watery part of blood.

platelets: very tiny pieces of cells that float in plasma and help form a clot to stop bleeding.

pulse: the throbbing you feel in your wrist or neck each time your heart beats.

red blood cells: the billions of tiny cells in your blood that contain hemoglobin.

stethoscope: an instrument used to listen to sounds inside your body.

symptoms: the fever, aches, or pains that you feel when you are ill.

tissues: groups of cells that are all the same and that form certain parts of your body, such as muscles or skin.

valves: tiny flaps inside your veins and your heart that keep blood from flowing backward.

veins: blood vessels that carry blood from your body back to your heart.

ventricle: one of the two lower chambers of your heart.

viruses: very tiny germs that can cause illnesses.

white blood cells: clear cells in your blood that help fight illnesses and infections.

More Books to Read

Blood. Body Books (series).
Anna Sandeman
(Copper Beech Books)

*The Circulatory System.
Human Body Systems* (series).
Helen Frost (Pebble Books)

*Hear Your Heart. Let's-Read-
And-Find-Out Science* (series).
Paul Showers (HarperCollins)

My Heart. My Body (series).
Kathy Furgang (Powerkids Press)

*Why Do Bruises Change Color:
And Other Questions About
Blood. Body Matters* (series).
Angela Royston (Heinemann)

Your Heart. Your Body (series).
Terri Degezelle
(Bridgestone Books)

Videos

Hemo the Magnificent.
(Rhino Home Video)

The Life of a Red Blood Cell.
(Aims Video)

Web Sites

BrainPOP: Circulatory System.
www.brainpop.com/health/
circulatory/blood/

Let's Learn About Your Heart!
www.mplsheartfoundation.
org/kids

Index